Discernment Companion

Study Guide, Journal, and Workbook

An in-depth study of the narrow gate and hard way that leads to life.

Carly Poe

Discernment Companion
Study Guide, Journal, and Workbook

First printing July 2013
Copyright © 2013 by Carly Poe

Unless otherwise indicated, all Scripture quotations are from the Holy Bible, English Standard Version ® (ESV®), copyright © 2001 by Crossway, a publishing ministry of Good Publishers. Used by permission. All rights reserved.

ISBN 978-0-9801768-2-7

Published by -
Wilderness Voice Publishing, LLC
Canon City, Colorado USA
www.wildernesspublishing.com

For additional information and curriculum catalog contact us by one of the following:

Message of the Cross International
PO Box 857
Canon City, CO 81215
888-575-9626
www.motci.com

MC Chapel Fellowship Training Center
The Abbey / St. Joseph's Bldg. Ste 102
Canon City, CO 81212
888-575-9626
www.mccfcanoncity.com

Introduction

Jesus taught, *"Enter by the narrow gate. For the gate is wide and the way is easy that leads to destruction, and those who enter by it are many. For the gate is narrow and the way is hard that leads to life, and those who find it are few"* (Matthew 7:13-14).

He also taught, *"Woe to you, scribes and Pharisees, hypocrites! For you are like whitewashed tombs, which outwardly appear beautiful, but within are full of dead people's bones and all uncleanliness. So you also outwardly appear righteous to others, but within you are full of hypocrisy and lawlessness"* (Matthew 23:27-28).

As far as where our focus in life should be, Jesus said, *"Abide in me, and I in you. As the branch cannot bear fruit by itself, unless it abides in the vine, neither can you, unless you abide in me"* (John 15:4).

We live in a church age where everything that Jesus taught is rarely talked about. It's rarely talked about because it is *hard*, and we as humans do not like to do hard things. We want things easy and we want them to make us feel better. Like sitting in a massage chair and just hitting a button, we want Jesus to melt all of our pain and worries away by a simple prayer. Often we feel like God owes us this because of "the work that we do for him." We would rather hear about God blessing us than God putting us through the discipline that is necessary for us to grow up in him. We want to hear the teachings that tickle our ears and give us warm fuzzies. If there is something in the Bible that we don't understand or that makes us feel uncomfortable, we flock to our favorite teacher to get their seminary coated interpretation of what Jesus teaches. And we tell ourselves that doing these things is perfectly fine because everyone is doing it. This mindset of taking the easy way to heaven has made us unable to see and discern evil within ourselves and others.

We are conditioned in the church to believe that if someone sits next to us in the pew, quotes a lot of Scripture and puts on the appearance of knowing Jesus, then they must be a "sincere Christian," altogether good and never should be thought about in any other way. But what we must be able to discern is the difference between those who simply follow Christ's name and those who *truly know him for who he is and everything that he taught.*

The enemy of our souls is wise. He is not a bumbling character dressed in red tights and carrying a pitchfork. Rather, he is a master of deception. Just as God has a plan to bring people into full relationship with him, Satan has a plan to deceive and destroy as many people as he can. Satan does this not only from outside of the church, but also from within the church. Paul understood and experienced this first hand. He writes of some so called Christians in Corinth, saying these things about them: *"And what I do I will continue to do, in order to undermine the claim of those who would like to claim that in their boasted mission they work on the same terms as we do. For such men are false apostles, deceitful workmen, disguising themselves as apostles of Christ. And no wonder, for even Satan disguises himself as an angel of light. So it is no surprise if his servants, also, disguise themselves as servants of righteousness. Their end will correspond to their deeds"* (2 Corinthians 11:12-15).

The basic understanding that Satan uses people within the church to carry out his plans is viewed by some as a hard-to-swallow heresy. People do not want to believe that *their* church could have evil people within it who work and live not for the Lord Jesus Christ but for themselves and for Satan. The enemy knows this, and so he does the best that he can to keep people mesmerized and fixated on how great they perceive their church to be and on their responsibility as a Christian to serve the church.

It is God's plan to use his *true* church to execute his righteousness and truth. But his true church is not the church that we see all over the media today. God's true church is made up of men and women who pledge their allegiance not to America, not to the latest and greatest teachers, and not to the biggest church in the city. God's true church consists of a people who have pledged their allegiance to Jesus Christ and to all that he taught, regardless of the price that they have to pay to do that.

God's true church belongs to a people who have heard Jesus words in Revelation 18 and have taken heed: *"Come out of her my people, lest you take part in her sins, lest you share in her plagues, for her sins are heaped high as heaven, and God has remembered her iniquities."* (Revelation 18:4-5).

In this passage, Jesus is referring to coming out of a church that has hidden the blood on their hands behind the distractions of their so-called worship services. The guilt of the modern church comes from the way that they continue to look the other way when it comes to calling evil what it really is and instead maintain an attitude of "the show must go on" — all too often at the expense of the people that they think they are serving.

Evil is not easy to discern—at first. Many become overwhelmed at the thought of the friend or acquaintance that they have attended church with for years really being an evil person. Denial is easier than facing the hard truth, and so many live in denial. They learn to ignore the promptings of the Holy Spirit and instead focus on the so-called good that the person has done. They let that become like an anesthetic, numbing out the truth of the pain that the good deeds of an evil person are just the disguise that the person uses to hide their true dark intentions.

Let me repeat that: the good deeds of an evil person are just the disguise that the person uses to hide their true dark intentions. So it makes sense that evil people choose to hide in churches everywhere. It is within the church that they can trumpet their good deeds for everyone to hear and easily keep up the façade of their sincerity.

One of the first things that people must begin to understand about evil and evil within the church is that there are varying degrees of it. As you read the book *Discernment* and work through the lessons in this workbook, you will gain an understanding of these different degrees of evil.

The evil that many of us encounter within the church has to do with people who are carnal Christians--that is, people who believe that they are operating in the power of the Holy Spirit but who are really operating in the power of their own flesh while they do work *for* Jesus and the church instead of allowing Jesus to work *through* them. The result of their work is carnal, leading to legalism, religiosity, and untimely death, never to life. *"For to set the mind on the flesh is death, but to set the mind on the Spirit is life and peace"* (Romans 8:6).

There are also deeper works of evil within the church today. There are servants of the enemy who have taken up residence within the church. Paul refers to them as people who disguise themselves as "angels of light." This tactic of the enemy, to send in his servants disguised as servants of Jesus, is one of his most deceiving tactics. The case studies that are explained throughout the book will give you deeper insight into these angel-of- light principalities and how they work.

The first step that every single one of us must take is learning to call evil what it is, with bravery and boldness, even when it hurts other people's feelings. Studying Charles Pretlow's work on discernment and utilizing this workbook and this discernment journal will help you to do that.

By truly examining what Christ taught, *especially the harder things that he taught,* and by going through countless life experiences, we have learned that evil often cloaks itself in decency, and Jesus demands that we learn how to discern between who is good and who is evil on his terms, not on our own. And while that is hard for us as humans, it is absolutely vital that we learn to do so. If we stay dull of hearing, hard of heart and empty of any true discernment, then it will be nearly impossible for us to stand, and truly impossible for us to be used of God, when it is going to matter the most.

This workbook on discernment is meant to help the sincere Christian learn to distinguish good from evil on Jesus' terms and live life according to that. The author of Hebrews wrote: *"But solid food is for the mature, for those who have their powers of discernment trained by constant practice to distinguish good from evil"* (Hebrews 5:13&14).

It is our goal that the lessons in this study guide serve as a tool to help the reader work with the Holy Spirit to discover and train their powers of discernment. May the reader of this work find the whole truth that Jesus taught in Scripture, the courage to embrace his complete truth, and the power that comes only from his Spirit to walk in true discernment, no matter the cost.

~Carly Poe

Table of Contents

Structure of Lessons in This Study Guide and Workbook

During my time with Youth with a Mission, I listened to a lesson where the teacher kept stressing that we, as Christians who want to work out our salvation, should learn to become readers, writers, and thinkers. I don't remember the name of the teacher who said that, but what he said impacted me so much that it has stuck with me for over ten years. In my own growth as a disciple of Christ, the more that I read, write, and think, the closer that I grow to Jesus. I believe that every person who truly wants to grow up into Jesus Christ must apply the disciplines of reading, writing, and thinking to their lives. The lessons in this study guide and workbook will follow that premise, in an effort to work out of the reader any passivity in their walk with Christ.

In Merriam Webster's online dictionary, the word *passive* is defined as: *(1)*: lacking in energy or will: lethargic; *(2)*: tending not to take an active or dominant part.

We have all been passive in our lives in certain areas. But taking a passive approach toward getting up on time in the morning is not the same as taking a passive approach to our walk with Christ. Getting up fifteen minutes late does not put us at risk eternally. Following Jesus idly does. Read the Parable of the Ten Virgins in Matthew 25 for proof of this. With a no tolerance attitude toward passivity with Christ, Paul wrote: *"Therefore, my beloved, as you have always obeyed, so now, not only as in my presence but much more in my absence, work out your own salvation with fear and trembling, for it is God who works in you, both to will and to work for his good pleasure."* (Philippians 2:12-13).

We are called to work out our own salvation with the guidance of the Holy Spirit. It is not something that we can do on our own, in the power of our own flesh. But as we rely on God for his direction and insight, he will help us to shed the passive approach that we often take with him and we will learn to work where, when and how he wants us to, as he guides us. In this process we will learn to *"grow up in every way into him who is the head, into Christ"* (Ephesians 4:15).

As you choose to complete the lessons found here, you will be asked to: 1) Read, 2) Write, 3) Think, and 4) Identify, all in an effort to aide and promote your true growth in Christ. You will be asked to read the book that this study guide is built for called *Discernment* by Charles Pretlow. You will also be asked to read numerous passages from the Bible. In writing, you will complete many different exercises to express what you are learning. You will be challenged to think critically and to identify principles throughout the Scriptures, as well as to reflect on your own life experiences and identify how those experiences relate to what you are learning. Throughout this whole process, it is our hope that those of you who choose to utilize this work will become trained in discernment and that you will grow up into Christ, living out what the author of Hebrews meant when he wrote: *"Therefore let us leave the elementary doctrine of Christ and go on to maturity"* (Hebrews 6:1).

Use the workshop notes section for each workshop you attend or for any DVD curriculum resource that becomes available from our expanding resource library catalog from Message of the Cross International or online at www.motci.com. Request current resource catalog from: MCI ~ PO Box 857 ~ Canon City, CO 81212.

Lesson 1

What Is Discernment?

Reminder: As you journey through these lessons, come prepared. Be ready to read. Be ready to write. Be ready to think. Be ready to identify. You will be challenged and encouraged by the Lord to truly grow up into his fullness!

1. Using the space provided below, define the word *discernment* in your own words.

Discernment:_____

_____

_____

_____

2. Read: Read Hebrews 5:11-14.

3. Write: What do you think the author of Hebrews is saying about discernment?

_____

_____

_____

_____

_____

_____

_____

_____

4. Think: Describe a time in your life when you had to use discernment and what happened. Or, if you cannot recall such a time, describe why you think that discernment is an important skill to have.

_____

_____

_____

_____

_____

_____

_____

_____

What Is Discernment?

> **A principle is a general or basic truth on which other truths or theories can be based.**
>
> (Source: Merriam Webster Dictionary online)

5. Read and Identify: It is vital to our growth as disciples of Jesus Christ that we learn to identify the principles that he and his Apostles teach us throughout the Bible. Read back through Hebrews 5:11-14. As you read, identify and write the principles that are found in the passage.

_____

_____

_____

_____

_____

6. Read, Write, and Think: Read chapter 1 of *Discernment*. Can you relate to any of the examples that the author gives in the chapter regarding discernment? Why can you relate to them?

_____

_____

_____

_____

_____

_____

_____

_____

_____

_____

_____

_____

_____

_____

_____

Lesson 2

Learning to See in the Dark

After reading chapter 1 of *Discernment* it should be apparent that the saint's darkest hour is truly coming upon us! There are some basic things about the end times that we must learn and allow to become part of our personal theology if we really want to walk in discernment and abide with Christ. The following questions will serve as a guide to help you learn to "see in the dark" of this hour and distinguish the truth from the lies about the end times.

1. Read and Write: Throughout the Gospels, Jesus talks about the end times. Find and list at least three Scriptures where Jesus talks about the end times.

_____

_____

_____

_____

2. Read, Write, Think, and Identify: There are different beliefs about the end times and when the rapture will happen. Through your own research, define the following two beliefs. List your sources at the end of your definitions.

Pre- Tribulation Rapture:

_____

_____

_____

_____

_____

_____

Post-Tribulation Rapture:

_____

_____

_____

_____

_____

_____

Learning to See in the Dark

3. Think and Identify: Which view, based on what Jesus says, is correct: Pre-Tribulation rapture or Post-Tribulation rapture? Explain why it is true.

_____

_____

_____

_____

_____

_____

_____

_____

4. Read, Write, Think, and Identify: Through your own research, define the Great Tribulation. Explain how to become prepared for it and why it is important to be prepared for it. List at least three Scriptures that back up your definition and explanations.

_____

_____

_____

_____

_____

_____

_____

_____

_____

_____

_____

_____

_____

Lesson 3

Praying for Strength to Endure

1. Read: Read what Jesus says in Luke 21:36.

2. Think and Write: In this life, there are many things that we can draw strength from. List at least four things that people use to gain emotional, physical, mental, and spiritual strength. Explain how people get strength from each of the things that you list.

_____

_____

_____

_____

_____

_____

True strength comes only from walking in right relationship with God.

3. Read, Write, and Think: Read Exodus 19:1-6. What does God ask the people to do in this passage?

_____

_____

_____

4. Think and Write: Obeying what God tells us to do in his Word, and obeying him when we hear his voice is a vital step in learning to walk in right relationship with him, which is the only thing that will truly enable us to endure the end times. Write your own definition of obedience below.

_____

_____

_____

_____

_____

Praying for Strength to Endure

5. Think and Write: How is our obedience to the Lord related to the strength that we have?

_____

_____

_____

_____

_____

_____

6. Write, Think, and Identify: When Jesus tells us in Luke 21:36 to pray that we may have strength, what kind of strength is he talking about?

_____

_____

_____

_____

_____

> **Right relationship with God means that we obey him and all that he teaches – no matter what the cost!!**

7. Write: Describe a time in your life when you obeyed God and how you gained strength from obeying him.

_____

_____

_____

_____

_____

_____

_____

Lesson 4

The Good, the Bad, and the Crazy

> "Evil will gain victory, even in America, when God's people forget, fall asleep, and ignore Christ and his teachings."
> - *Discernment*, chapter 2

1. Read: Read chapter 2 of *Discernment.*

2. Write, Think, and Identify: Define what "good evil" is. Give two biblical examples, with Scripture references, of people who are good evil.

_____

_____

_____

_____

_____

3. Write, Think, and Identify: Define what "bad evil" is. Through your own research, give two examples of people in society who are bad evil.

_____

_____

_____

_____

_____

4. Write, Think, and Identify: Define what "crazy evil" is. Through your own research, give two examples of people in society who are crazy evil.

_____

_____

_____

_____

_____

The Good, the Bad, and the Crazy

5. Write and Think: What are the main differences between the good evil, the bad evil, and the crazy evil?

_____

_____

_____

_____

_____

6. Read and Write: Read 2 Thessalonians 3:2. Explain what Paul means by saying "not all have faith." How does what he says relate to people who are good evil, bad evil, and crazy evil?

_____

_____

_____

_____

_____

_____

_____

_____

_____

7. Read, Write, Think, and Identify: Read through the lists of characteristics of good evil, bad evil and crazy evil people. Have you ever had experiences with these types of people? Describe your experience or experiences below.

_____

_____

_____

_____

_____

_____

_____

_____

Lesson 5

The Nature and Characteristics of Evil

A person's nature has to do with their inherent traits, their disposition and their temperament.	A person's character has to do with their morals and ethics and the choices that they make as a result of those morals and ethics.

1. Read and Write: Read John 8:39-47. What is the devil's character? List at least two characteristics of his nature.

_____

_____

_____

_____

2. Think and Write: Who was Jesus talking to in this passage? How religious do you think they were?

_____

_____

_____

3. Think and Write: Who did Jesus say that these people's father was?

_____

4. Write, Think, and Identify: Why did Jesus say that these people had the devil's character? What was the will of these people, according to Jesus?

_____

_____

_____

_____

_____

_____

The Nature and Characteristics of Evil

> **Principle: Understanding evil is impossible apart from the Bible's explanation and Christ's teachings.**

5. Think and Write: In an attempt to get people to develop a nature and character like his, the devil uses a process that Pretlow refers to as "demonic fracking of the human psyche." Explain this process in your own words.

_____

_____

_____

_____

_____

_____

_____

_____

_____

_____

6. Write: The devil works to break the personal spirit of individuals. List at least three Scriptures that talk about how a person's personal spirit can be broken.

_____

_____

7. Think and Write: There are sinners who have done evil, which is a category that we all fall into. There is also human evil that is instituted by the devil. Explain the difference between the two.

_____

_____

_____

_____

_____

Lesson 6

Christian Sorcery and False Ministries

1. Read: Read chapter 3 of *Discernment*.

2. Think and Write: Describe what Christian sorcery is. Can you think of a time when you knew of someone practicing Christian sorcery, or perhaps a time when you unknowingly practiced it yourself?

_____

_____

_____

_____

_____

_____

_____

_____

_____

_____

_____

_____

3. Write, Think, and Identify: In chapter three, Pretlow talks about our fallen nature, and due to that nature, how we often idolize other people. We "make them responsible for our well-being, happiness, and often make them or allow them to be responsible for our salvation, even putting them in the place of God." Have you ever done this in your own life? Write about your experience and explain how doing this relates to Christian sorcery.

_____

_____

_____

_____

_____

_____

_____

_____

_____

_____

Christian Sorcery and False Ministries

4. Read, Write, Think, and Identify: Along with the practice of Christian sorcery, carnal church programs and carnal church slogans often become a way for us to do our own will, and even Satan's will, instead of God's will. Read Hebrews 5:11-14 again. How do we, as Christians, buy into these programs and slogans, and how do they make us "dull of hearing?"

_____
_____
_____
_____
_____
_____
_____
_____
_____

5. Read, Write, and Identify: Read through the list of teachings in *Discernment* (pages 110-112) that many ministries use. Have you ever been involved in a church or a ministry that teaches these things? Describe what the ministry or church taught and if you believed what they taught or not. Explain why these teachings are false.

_____
_____
_____
_____
_____
_____
_____
_____
_____
_____
_____

The Gates of Hell

1. Think and Write: What are "the gates of hell"?

_____

2. Read, Write, and Think: Read Matthew 26:20-25. Why did Jesus allow Judas to be with the disciples for so long even though he knew that Judas would betray him? What was he showing them about the gates of hell?

_____

_____

_____

3. Think and Write: How does a person become a gate of hell?

_____

_____

_____

_____

4. Think and Write: How does our submission to the Lord and his work and discipline in our lives affect the power of the demonic in our lives?

_____

_____

_____

_____

_____

_____

_____

> **Principle: The gates of hell are people who have given themselves over to the will of Satan.**

The Gates of Hell

5. Think and Write: Sadly, many so-called Christian leaders become false leaders as they submit to their own desires, the desires of their congregation and ultimately the devil's desires, instead of Jesus' teachings. Many of these leaders become like Simon the Magician as described in Acts 8:18-23. Read this passage and explain what "Simon-the-Magician Christian leadership" is, expounding on how Simon's heart was not right before God, and how having a corrupt heart affects your ability to lead God's people in God's way.

_____

_____

_____

_____

_____

_____

_____

_____

_____

_____

6. Think and Write: The gates of hell and false leaders work together to deceive people through false deliverance ministries. According to what you read in chapter 3, what is the "common thread" in false deliverance ministries?

_____

_____

_____

7. Think and Write: What determines the true authenticity of a leader and a ministry?

_____

_____

_____

_____

_____

Psuchē and *Zōē*

1. Read: Read chapter 4 of *Discernment*.

2. Read, Write, and Think: Read Galatians 5:19-21. What is the *psuchē* life? Describe the characteristics of it and how it affects our relationships.

_____
_____
_____
_____
_____
_____
_____
_____
_____
_____
_____
_____
_____

3. Read, Write, and Think: Read John 10:10 and Galatians 5:22- 23. What is the *zōē* life? Describe the characteristics of it and how it affects our relationships.

_____
_____
_____
_____
_____
_____
_____
_____
_____
_____
_____

Psuchē and *Zōē*

4. Think and Write: In the *psuchē* life, where does a person's sense of well-being come from?

_____

_____

_____

5. Think and Write: In the *zōē* life, where does a person's sense of well-being come from?

_____

_____

_____

_____

6. Read, Write, Think, and Identify: When we live for the *psuchē* life as a Christian, often we fall for the lie of "cheap grace." What is cheap grace? How does living for the *psuchē* life make us susceptible to it?

_____

_____

_____

_____

_____

_____

_____

_____

_____

_____

_____

_____

_____

_____

_____

_____

_____

Lesson 9

Wheat, Weeds, and Devotion to Deceitful Spirits

> **Principle: Because of the lies of the false, people will devote themselves to deceitful spirits and to the teachings of demons.**
> **(See 1 Timothy 4:1-2)**

1. Read, Write, and Think: Read Matthew 13:24-30. Who are the "wheat" that Jesus describes here? Who are the "weeds"?

_____

_____

_____

_____

_____

2. Think and Write: Why does Jesus allow the weeds to grow with the wheat? What lessons is he teaching the wheat through this process?

_____

_____

_____

_____

_____

_____

_____

_____

3. Think and Write: How do the lies of the false (the weeds) influence people to devote themselves to deceitful spirits and to the teachings of demons?

_____

_____

_____

_____

_____

Wheat, Weeds, and Devotion to Deceitful Spirits

4. Read, Write, and Think: There are many ways that the false will pervert the truth and the grace of God as they live among and go to church with the true believers in Christ. Read Jude 1:4. What does it mean to pervert the grace of God into sensuality? Have you ever experienced a perverted grace of God? Describe your experience here.

_____

_____

_____

_____

_____

_____

_____

_____

5. Think and Write: Who are the" elect" that Jesus talks about?

_____

_____

_____

6. Think and Write: Deceived Christians, who have bought into the lies of the weeds, must arrive at a paramount truth. What is that truth?

_____

_____

_____

> "Christ did not and will not protect a people who speak his
> name, yet live apart from him and his lordship."
> – *Discernment*, chapter 4

False, Super, Pseudo, and Personality Christians

NOTE: Throughout chapter 5 in the book *Discernment*, and also throughout the lessons developed from chapter 5 in this workbook, the terms *false apostle, super apostle, pseudo Christian* and *personality leader* all refer to the same type of person. You will discover what type of person that is as you read the chapter and work though these lessons.

1. Read: Read chapter 5 of *Discernment*.

2. Read, Write, Think, and Identify: Read 2 Corinthians 11:1-15. How do you determine if someone is a *false apostle*?

_____

_____

_____

_____

_____

3. Write, Think, and Identify: What is a *personality leader* and what is the root problem with personality leaders?

_____

_____

_____

_____

_____

4. Think and Write: What work does Satan do through personality leaders?

_____

_____

_____

_____

_____

_____

_____

False, Super, Pseudo, and Personality Christians

> False, Super, Pseudo and Personality Christians buy into many deceptions. A basic but lethal deception that they buy into is a false belief about how sanctification works!

> False Belief: The heart and spirit of a believer is completely transformed at the time of rebirth.

> The Truth: The born again experience is just the beginning of a Biblical process of cleansing, purifying, renewing and transforming the heart, spirit and the mind. This process is called sanctification.

5. Read and Think: Read Jeremiah 17:9 and Matthew 15:18-20. Where do evil thoughts and actions come from?

_____

_____

6. Read, Write, Think, and Identify: Read through Joyce Meyer's "12 Power Thoughts" (_Discernment_ page 161). Have any of these power thoughts ever helped you? Describe your experience below.

_____

_____

_____

_____

_____

_____

_____

7. Read, Write, Think, and Identify: Read John 3:5-8 and Romans 7:15-25. What in us must be transformed before our minds can be renewed? What is our responsibility in our own transformation process?

_____

_____

_____

_____

_____

_____

Lesson 11

Churchianity

Churchianity is a word for an unusual and excessive attachment to the practices and interests of a certain church. Such an attachment places more emphasis on the habits and institutional traditions of church life than the Christian teachings that are promoted in the church.
(ask.com)

1. Think and Write: What is a carnal dynamic relationship network?

_____

_____

_____

2. Think and Write: Describe the dynamics of churchianity and how it affects the relationships and the lives of the people that are stuck in it.

_____

_____

_____

_____

_____

_____

_____

_____

_____

_____

_____

_____

_____

3. Think and Write: What does churchianity cause leaders to become enthralled with?

_____

_____

_____

_____

_____

Churchianity

> "New comers and God seekers are now attracted by marketing slogans, not drawn by the Holy Spirit."
> – *Discernment*, chapter 5

4. Think and Write: How can you tell if you have an attachment to a church, a ministry or a favorite leader, but not to the true Christ?

_____

_____

_____

_____

_____

5. Read, Write, and Think: Read Galatians 1:6-10. The practices of those churches that are stuck in churchianity please other people rather than pleasing God. Have you ever experienced a situation where a church was more focused on pleasing other people than on pleasing God? Describe it here.

_____

_____

_____

_____

_____

_____

_____

_____

_____

_____

_____

_____

_____

Lesson 12

The Soul and the Spirit

The *soul* is essentially the mind and the heart of a person. It continues to grow and develop throughout a person's life.

The *spirit* of a person is intended to be the dwelling place of the Holy Spirit, by God's design. It is meant to be dormant until the Holy Spirit awakens it at the time of rebirth- (truly coming to the knowledge of who Jesus Christ is and what he has done for humanity.)

1. Read: Read chapter 6 of *Discernment*.

2. Think and Write: According to what you read in chapter 6, what is the difference between our soul and our spirit?

_____

_____

_____

_____

3. Think and Write: According to God's desire for us, when is our spirit supposed to be awakened, and who is supposed to wake it up?

_____

_____

_____

4. Think and Write: What is the difference between knowing of God and being born of God?

_____

_____

_____

5. Think and Write: What is the "life exchange program" between us and Jesus Christ?

_____

_____

_____

The Soul and the Spirit

6. Read, Write, and Think: Just as God has a plan for our personal spirit, so does Satan. Satan works hard to awaken our spirit before God plans for it to be awakened. Satan uses wounds that happen to our spirit to accomplish this. Read Proverbs 15:4 and explain how Satan can use perverse words that are spoken to us to awaken our spirit prematurely and then wound or break it.

_____

_____

_____

_____

_____

_____

7. Think and Write: What must we do so that our personal spirit can be brought back to God?

_____

_____

_____

_____

_____

8. Read, Write, and Think: Read 2 Corinthians 7:1 and Hebrews 4:12. Why is it important to allow the Holy Spirit to separate and heal our personal spirit and our soul? What damage can our personal spirit do to others when it is still wounded, defiled and intertwined with our emotions and our selfishness?

_____

_____

_____

_____

_____

_____

_____

_____

_____

Lesson 13

Spiritual Powers of the Flesh

1. Think and Write: Based on what you have just read in chapter 6, write a brief summary of what the spiritual powers of the flesh are.

_____

_____

_____

_____

_____

_____

_____

2. Read, Write, and Think: Read James 3:14-16. What in us can boost the power of our spirits and negatively affect the lives of others? What are the results in the lives of others if we practice the spiritual powers of the flesh?

_____

_____

_____

_____

_____

_____

_____

3. Think and Write: What is the primary reason that so many believers in Christ become recipients of counterfeiting demons?

_____

_____

_____

> **"True Christians learn to discern spirits and worship God by the Spirit of God, not in the power of their own spirit."** -- *Discernment,* chapter 6

Spiritual Powers of the Flesh

4. Think and Write: How is the activity of evil counterfeit spirits related to false gift manifestations in a Christian's life? How do evil counterfeit spirits become active in a Christian's life?

_____

_____

_____

_____

5. Think and Write: How does the belief that all Christians need to be baptized in the Holy Spirit and speak in tongues, in order to have fullness of life in Christ, make them vulnerable to counterfeiting spirits and empty manifestations?

_____

_____

_____

_____

_____

_____

6. Read, Write, Think, and Identify: Read through the symptoms of a demon boosted human spirit attack (*Discernment* pages 223 – 224). Describe a time when you felt one or more of these symptoms, whether or not you suspected you were under attack and what you did about it.

_____

_____

_____

_____

_____

_____

_____

_____

_____

Lesson 14

True Leadership

1. Read: Read chapter 7 of *Discernment*.

2. Think and Write: What is required of leaders who truly want to disciple others?

_____

_____

_____

3. Write, Think, and Identify: List at least five qualities of a Christ- like leader and explain why you think these qualities are important for a true leader to have.

_____

_____

_____

_____

_____

_____

_____

_____

_____

4. Think and Write: What does it mean to seek the *full* love of God, toward God, others and self?

_____

_____

_____

_____

5. Think and Write: What is the fivefold work of servant leaders?

_____

_____

_____

_____

_____

True Leadership

> "Leadership must exert most of their effort in confronting God's people- not the sinner and an evil, wicked culture."
> – *Discernment*, chapter 7

6. Think and Write: What is leadership idolatry? What were the results of it in Moses' life? What are the results of it in people's lives today?

_____

_____

_____

_____

_____

_____

7. Write, Think, and Identify: Look up and define the word *insubordinate*. Then, think of a time that you dealt with an insubordinate person and describe what happened.

_____

_____

_____

_____

_____

_____

_____

_____

8. Think and Write: In today's modern church, what are leadership qualities falsely measured by?

_____

_____

_____

_____

Lesson 15

Growth in Christ

1. Think and Write: How are the harder teachings of Jesus Christ like an antiseptic to the soul and the spirit of a person?

_____

_____

_____

_____

_____

_____

2. Think and Write: What is the real nature of false teachings? What does it do to those who follow false teachings?

_____

_____

_____

_____

_____

3. Think and Write: How does God use the devil and the trials of our lives to break our denial?

_____

_____

_____

_____

_____

4. Think and Write: Define godly grief and worldly grief and explain the difference between the two.

_____

_____

_____

_____

Growth in Christ

5. Think and Write: Describe in detail the general phases of maturing. Use pages 251- 254 in *Discernment* as a guide.

_____
_____
_____
_____
_____
_____
_____
_____
_____
_____

6. Write, Think, and Identify: List five principles of growing up into Christ and explain how each principle works.

_____
_____
_____
_____
_____
_____
_____
_____
_____
_____
_____
_____
_____
_____
_____

Lesson 16

Get Your Theology Right

Theology: the study of religious faith, practice, and experience;
especially: **the study of God and of God's relation to the world.**
(merriam-webster.com)

1. Read: Read chapter 8 of *Discernment*.

2. Think and Write: In order to relate to God correctly and understand how to develop our powers of discernment, it is absolutely vital that we get our theology right. What should our theology be based on if we want it to be correct?

_____

_____

_____

3. Think and Write: What is "junk theology" and what does it create?

_____

_____

_____

4. Read, Write, and Think: Read Luke 14: 27-33. What does it mean to count the cost of following the true Christ? How should counting this cost affect our theology?

_____

_____

_____

_____

_____

_____

_____

_____

_____

_____

Get Your Theology Right

> "The only theology that is true, practical and approved by God comes from Christ -- from all the teachings of Christ, revealed and applied with proper understanding through the person of Christ."
> -- *Discernment*, chapter 8

5. Think and Write: How should we study the Old Testament?

_____

_____

_____

6. Think and Write: What is the difference between *knowing* Jesus Christ and *knowing of* Jesus Christ?

_____

_____

_____

_____

7. Think and Write: What does it mean to be righteous in your own eyes? How does Satan use being righteous in our own eyes against us?

_____

_____

_____

_____

8. Think and Write: For many false teachers, the grace of God has become a theological license to baby and make excuses for Christians. How does this keep churches immature?

_____

_____

_____

_____

_____

Lesson 17

Study the Word

In order to grow up into Christ and develop our powers of discernment, we must learn to utilize the Bible. The following exercises will help you to become disciplined in studying the Word of God.

1. Read, Write, and Think: Read Hebrews 5:7-10. How does going through suffering develop a true, godly fear in us?

_____

_____

_____

_____

_____

_____

_____

_____

2. Read, Write, and Think: Read Job 33:14-22 and Job 33:29-30. Explain how God uses our suffering to break our self-righteousness and our denial.

_____

_____

_____

_____

_____

_____

_____

_____

_____

_____

_____

Study the Word

3. Read, Write, and Think: Read 1 John 2:15-17. Explain what the desires of the flesh, the desires of the eyes and pride in possessions are. Explain how the world and these desires are passing away, and what it means to abide forever if we do the will of God.

_____

_____

_____

_____

_____

_____

_____

_____

_____

_____

_____

_____

4. Read, Write, and Think: Read Hebrews 12:1-11. Explain what it means and how we, as true Christians, are supposed to view and receive the discipline of the Lord.

_____

_____

_____

_____

_____

_____

_____

_____

_____

_____

_____

_____

_____

_____

Lesson 18

Aspects of the Battle

> "When the hour of evil hits us with the force of darkness, we become shaken free from living in the world haphazardly."
> – *Discernment*, chapter 9

1. Read: Read chapter 9 of *Discernment*.

2. Think and Write: Explain how vacillating about when the rapture occurs can be a damning thing to do.

_____

_____

3. Think and Write: Whose wrath will we have to endure during the Great Tribulation?

_____

4. Think and Write: Explain why the belief that converting the world to Christianity in order to "save it" is erroneous and will not work.

_____

_____

_____

_____

_____

5. Read, Write, and Think: Read Revelation 18:4-8. How is America becoming more and more like the Great Babylon of the book of Revelation?

_____

_____

_____

_____

_____

_____

Aspects of the Battle

6. Read, Write, and Think: Read the quote below. Then, explain what emotional irrationalism is and how it will affect people in the coming chaos of the Great Tribulation.

> *"Logical and rational thinking will be replaced by hatred and emotional irrationalism as the divide between the wicked and the righteous widens. "- Discernment,* chapter 9

_____
_____
_____
_____
_____
_____

7. Read, Write, and Think: Read 2 Peter 2, Jude 1:10-19, James 3:14-16, and James 4:1-10. Based on what you read, list at least five characteristics of a wounded, unstable Christian and five characteristics of a false Christian. Then, explain the main differences between the two.

_____
_____
_____
_____
_____
_____
_____
_____

8. Think and Write: How can our mistakes in the battle become precious nuggets of insight, wisdom and grace?

_____
_____
_____
_____
_____

Lesson 19

Learning to Abide

1. Write: Using a dictionary, write an in-depth definition of the word *abide*.

_____

_____

_____

2. Think and Write: We learn to abide in many things as humans. List at least three things that we can abide in as humans and explain how and why we abide in these things.

_____

_____

_____

_____

_____

_____

3. Think and Write: Read John 15:1-11. Explain in your own words what Jesus is saying here. Explain how we can learn to abide in him.

_____

_____

_____

_____

_____

_____

_____

_____

4. Think and Write: Why is learning to abide in Jesus important?

_____

_____

_____

_____

_____

Learning to Abide

5. Think and Write: Explain how abiding in Jesus will affect the way that we handle the coming chaos of the Great Tribulation. How will abiding in him help us? How will not abiding in him harm us?

_____

_____

_____

_____

_____

_____

6. Write, Think, and Identify: According to John 15, what are the positive effects of learning to abide in nothing but Jesus?

_____

_____

_____

_____

_____

7. Read, Write, and Think: Read Matthew 7: 24-27. What does it mean to abide in Jesus' words? Explain in your own words what Jesus is saying here about abiding in him and in what he teaches.

_____

_____

_____

_____

_____

_____

> "Because you have kept my word about patient endurance, I will keep you from the hour of trial that is coming on the whole world, to try those who dwell on the earth. I am coming soon. Hold fast what you have, so that no one may seize your crown." – Revelation 3:10-11

Patient Endurance

"But recall the former days when, after you were enlightened, you endured a hard struggle with sufferings, sometimes being publicly exposed to reproach and affliction, and sometimes being partners with those so treated. For you had compassion on those in prison, and you joyfully accepted the plundering of your property, since you knew that you yourselves had a better possession and an abiding one. Therefore do not throw away your confidence, which has a great reward. For you have need of endurance, so that when you have done the will of God you may receive what is promised. For, 'Yet a little while, and the coming one will come and will not delay; but my righteous one shall live by faith, and if he shrinks back, my soul has no pleasure in him.' But we are not of those who shrink back and are destroyed, but of those who have faith and preserve their souls" (Hebrews 10:32-39).

We pray that this work on discernment has enlightened you to a deeper understanding of the times that we are in, to the deceitful tactics of the enemy during these times, and to the call of Christ to do the work necessary to grow up into him and abide with him—so that you may be able to endure the troubles that are coming.

If there is a paramount key to withstanding battles with the enemy and with those who do his will, that key is summed up in this phrase: patient endurance.

Patient endurance can be defined as—the ability and the willingness to withstand prolonged, stressful situations, calmly and without complaining. This is exactly what we all need to be able to do, if we hope to be able to stand as true servants of Christ in the end.

We tend to think that the events that will require our patient endurance are of a grand scale and will happen later on. We do this because it makes life easier on us in the here and now. It also causes us to live with a "later on" attitude in our walk with Christ and dulls our understanding of the importance of growing up into him. We will study the Bible later on, listen to his voice later on, and if we are feeling really ambitious, let God begin to deal with us and with our heart issues later on.

Later on is too late and our life with Christ was never meant to be easy! The things that the Lord wants us to patiently endure have much more to do with daily life than they do with a detached idea of extreme chaos that we will somehow have to get through at some point in time. The Lord requires us to learn how to suffer. We will suffer as we hear from the Lord our true heart's intentions and discover how ugly our flesh is. But we will suffer even more if we deny our ugliness and refuse to go through the process of dying to our flesh so that we can learn to abide in nothing but the Lord. We will suffer as we begin to make changes in our relationships that are unhealthy and that have become idols in our lives. And we will suffer as those who do not like the changes that we are making vehemently come against us. In the midst of all of this, we have a choice to make: we can stand with the Lord and do what he is telling us to do, or we can listen to what other people are saying against us and back out of what God wants for us. The choice is ours. The consequences are eternal.

The discernment journal on the following pages is meant to help you have a place to write down your daily struggles, victories and discoveries as you walk through this process of patient endurance with the Lord. As you reflect on what you have written, you will have a testimony to encourage yourself as doubt creeps in, and also a testimony to encourage others as they begin the same journey of patient endurance that you have.

May the courage and reassurance of the Lord fill you as you remember that as his true children *"we are not of those who shrink back and are destroyed, but of those who have faith and preserve their souls"* (Hebrews 10:39).

~Carly Poe

Discernment Devotional Day 1: *"About this we have much to say, and it is hard to explain, since you have become dull of hearing. For though by this time you ought to be teachers, you need someone to teach you again the basic principles of the oracles of God. You need milk, not solid food, for everyone who lives on milk is unskilled in the word of righteousness, since he is a child. But solid food is for the mature, for those who have their powers of discernment trained by constant practice to distinguish good from evil"* (Hebrews 5:11-14).

In what areas of your life are you still "drinking milk?" What growth with the Lord have you been avoiding and why have you been avoiding it? Get alone with God and figure it out. Your life literally depends on it.

Use the space below to write about what Hebrews 5:11-14 means to you. How is God speaking to you through it?

_____

_____

_____

_____

_____

_____

_____

_____

_____

_____

_____

_____

_____

_____

_____

_____

_____

_____

_____

_____

_____

_____

Discernment Devotional Day 2: *"Not only that, but we rejoice in our sufferings, knowing that suffering produces endurance, and endurance produces character, and character produces hope, and hope does not put us to shame, because God's love has been poured into our hearts through the Holy Spirit who has been given to us"*(Romans 5:3-5).

Suffering is generally viewed as a bad thing. The process that the Apostle Paul explains here gives us proper understanding of what our suffering can grow into, if we allow God to teach us through it. Are you letting the suffering in your life have the full effect that God wants it to?

Use the space below to write about what Romans 5:3-5 means to you. How is God speaking to you through it?

_____

_____

_____

_____

_____

_____

_____

_____

_____

_____

_____

_____

_____

_____

_____

_____

_____

_____

_____

_____

_____

_____

_____

_____

_____

_____

Discernment Devotional Day 3: *"Enter by the narrow gate. For the gate is wide and the way is easy that leads to destruction, and those who enter by it are many. For the gate is narrow and the way is hard that leads to life, and those who find it are few"* (Matthew 7:13-14).

Learning to enter by the narrow gate requires that we live our lives by *all* that Jesus taught, even when it hurts so much that we think we can't go on! Ask God to teach you how to enter by the narrow gate and live his way, even when it is difficult. If you don't, then you are headed for destruction.

Use the space below to write about what Matthew 7:13-14 means to you. How is God speaking to you through it?

_____
_____
_____
_____
_____
_____
_____
_____
_____
_____
_____
_____
_____
_____
_____
_____
_____
_____
_____
_____
_____
_____
_____
_____
_____
_____
_____

Discernment Devotional Day 4: *"Finally, brothers, pray for us, that the word of the Lord may speed ahead and be honored, as happened among you, and that we may be delivered from wicked and evil men. For not all have faith"* (2 Thessalonians 3:1-2).

Not all people have faith in God. We tend to think of those people who don't have faith in God as people who believe other religions. But evil and wicked people can act like they believe in God. They can use their false faith as a disguise to do wicked things. Evil people who act holy are a reality that we must learn how to discern. Ask the Lord to help you develop the skill of true discernment!

Use the space below to write about what 2 Thessalonians 3:1-2 means to you. How is God speaking to you through it?

_____

_____

_____

_____

_____

_____

_____

_____

_____

_____

_____

_____

_____

_____

_____

_____

_____

_____

_____

_____

_____

_____

_____

_____

_____

_____

_____

Discernment Devotional Day 5: *"If any of you lacks wisdom, let him ask God, who gives generously to all without reproach, and it will be given him. But let him ask in faith, with no doubting, for the one who doubts is like a wave of the sea that is driven and tossed by the wind. For that person must not suppose that he will receive anything from the Lord; he is a double-minded man, unstable in all his ways"* (James 1:5-8).

Our doubt is something that we must honestly deal with. When we doubt the Lord but still try to push forward in our own strength, then we will be tossed around. We will never be stable in the Lord. We must accept the fact that we are double-minded; part of us loves God but part of us wants to live by our own agenda. We have to allow God to deal with our double-mindedness. Get honest before God about your doubts and your double-mindedness. Then let him take you through his process of healing. Only then will your prayers be answered according to his will, not your own.

Use the space below to write about what James 1:5-8 means to you. How is God speaking to you through it?

_____

_____

_____

_____

_____

_____

_____

_____

_____

_____

_____

_____

_____

_____

_____

_____

_____

_____

_____

_____

_____

_____

Discernment Devotional Day 6: *"Today, if you hear his voice, do not harden your hearts as in the rebellion"* (Hebrews 3:15).

Do not condemn yourself before God when he tells you something that you don't want to hear. Accept his encouraging warning as an opportunity to change. When we see our own issues and deal with them, we are then able to discern issues in others and convey truth.

Use the space below to write about what Hebrews 3:15 means to you. How is God speaking to you through it?

_____

_____

_____

_____

_____

_____

_____

_____

_____

_____

_____

_____

_____

_____

_____

_____

_____

_____

_____

_____

_____

_____

_____

_____

_____

_____

_____

_____

Discernment Devotional Day 7: *"Either make the tree good and its fruit good, or make the tree bad and its fruit bad, for the tree is known by its fruit. You brood of vipers! How can you speak good, when you are evil? For out of the abundance of the heart the mouth speaks. The good person out of his good treasure brings forth good, and the evil person out of his evil treasure brings forth evil. I tell you, on the day of judgment people will give account for every careless word they speak, for by your words you will be justified, and by your words you will be condemned"* (Matthew 12:33-37).

Jesus knew that there are good people in the world and there are evil people in the world. He was especially against people who on the inside were evil, but spoke as if they were good. Evil likes to cloak itself in decency. One of the key tools in learning true discernment is being able to look beyond who a person says he is with his words and into who he says he is with his actions. His true character will come out, and you will see him or her for who he truly is, if you are in tune with God and what he wants you to see about that person.

Use the space below to write about what Matthew 12:33-37 means to you. How is God speaking to you through it?

_____
_____
_____
_____
_____
_____
_____
_____
_____
_____
_____
_____
_____
_____
_____
_____
_____
_____
_____
_____
_____
_____

Discernment Devotional Day 8: *"Indeed, all who desire to live a godly life in Christ Jesus will be persecuted, while evil people and impostors will go on from bad to worse, deceiving and being deceived. But as for you, continue in what you have learned and have firmly believed, knowing from whom you learned it and how from childhood you have been acquainted with the sacred writings, which are able to make you wise for salvation through faith in Christ Jesus"* (2 Timothy 3:12-15).

Paul's words of encouragement to Timothy are ones that we can take to heart today! It is true that everyone who desires to live a godly life *in Jesus-not in the works they do or in the teachers that they listen to-* will be persecuted. Learning to abide in Jesus will be hard, but it will be worth it. Being persecuted because you trust in Jesus for who he really is, is part of the process that leads to true salvation. Those who teach that you will not suffer as a true disciple of Christ are deceived and are teaching a deception.

Use the space below to write about what 2 Timothy 3:12-15 means to you. How is God speaking to you through it?

_____

_____

_____

_____

_____

_____

_____

_____

_____

_____

_____

_____

_____

_____

_____

_____

_____

_____

_____

_____

_____

_____

_____

_____

_____

Discernment Devotional Day 9: *"I appeal to you, brothers, to watch out for those who cause divisions and create obstacles contrary to the doctrine that you have been taught; avoid them. For such persons do not serve our Lord Christ, but their own appetites, and by smooth talk and flattery they deceive the hearts of the naïve. For your obedience is known to all, so that I rejoice over you, but I want you to be wise as to what is good and innocent as to what is evil. The God of peace will soon crush Satan under your feet. The grace of our Lord Jesus Christ be with you"* (Romans 16:17-20).

Paul is giving some very important instructions here. As you grow in your ability to discern, you will learn who to avoid and how to avoid them. Always ask yourself- Is this person flattering me? If they are, ask yourself why, and what attracts you to people who flatter you in the first place. Do not be deceived by flattery!

Use the space below to write about what Romans 16:17-20 means to you. How is God speaking to you through it?

_____
_____
_____
_____
_____
_____
_____
_____
_____
_____
_____
_____
_____
_____
_____
_____
_____
_____
_____
_____
_____
_____

Discernment Devotional Day 10: *"Not everyone who says to me, 'Lord, Lord,' will enter the kingdom of heaven, but the one who does the will of my Father who is in heaven. On that day many will say to me, 'Lord, Lord, did we not prophesy in your name, and cast out demons in your name, and do many mighty works in your name?' And then will I declare to them, 'I never knew you; depart from me, you workers of lawlessness'"* (Matthew 7:21-23).

In this passage, Jesus is making a statement about what will happen to people who follow him in the power of their own flesh. We must learn to distinguish between the power that comes from our own flesh and the power that comes from God. Always ask yourself- Are these works that I am doing based on God's will for me, or on my own desire to be seen by other people as someone who works for God?

Use the space below to write about what Matthew 7:21-23 means to you. How is God speaking to you through it?

_____
_____
_____
_____
_____
_____
_____
_____
_____
_____
_____
_____
_____
_____
_____
_____
_____
_____
_____
_____
_____
_____
_____
_____

Discernment Devotional Day 11: *"Who is wise and understanding among you? By his good conduct let him show his works in the meekness of wisdom. But if you have bitter jealousy and selfish ambition in your hearts, do not boast and be false to the truth. This is not the wisdom that comes down from above, but is earthly, unspiritual, demonic. For where jealousy and selfish ambition exist, there will be disorder and every vile practice"* (James 3:13-16).

Do you have bitter jealousy and selfish ambition in your heart? If you do, admit it to God and let him help you figure out why. The worst thing that you can do is become boastful in your denial of your heart's true condition. Denial is demonic and boasting about it makes you a person who lives in falsehood. What kind of person do you want to be?

Use the space below to write about what James 3:13-16 means to you. How is God speaking to you through it?

_____
_____
_____
_____
_____
_____
_____
_____
_____
_____
_____
_____
_____
_____
_____
_____
_____
_____
_____
_____
_____
_____
_____
_____
_____

Discernment Devotional Day 12: *"Consider him who endured from sinners such hostility against himself, so that you may not grow weary or fainthearted. In your struggle against sin you have not yet resisted to the point of shedding your blood. And have you forgotten the exhortation that addresses you as sons?*

> *'My son, do not regard lightly the discipline of the Lord,*
>   *nor be weary when reproved by him.*
> *For the Lord disciplines the one he loves,*
>   *and chastises every son whom he receives.'*

It is for discipline that you have to endure. God is treating you as sons. For what son is there whom his father does not discipline? If you are left without discipline, in which all have participated, then you are illegitimate children and not sons. Besides this, we have had earthly fathers who disciplined us and we respected them. Shall we not much more be subject to the Father of spirits and live? For they disciplined us for a short time as it seemed best to them, but he disciplines us for our good, that we may share his holiness. For the moment all discipline seems painful rather than pleasant, but later it yields the peaceful fruit of righteousness to those who have been trained by it" (Hebrews 12:3-11).

There isn't much that can be said that puts it better than this passage in Hebrews does. So study it and receive the discipline of the Lord in your life!

Use the space below to write about what Hebrews 12:3-11 means to you. How is God speaking to you through it?

_____
_____
_____
_____
_____
_____
_____
_____
_____
_____
_____
_____
_____
_____
_____
_____
_____
_____
_____
_____

| Date: | **Workshop Notes** | Session Number: |

Workshop Title _____   Speaker _____

Use this blank page and the pages following it to take notes at the Discernment workshop and also to take notes as you read the book *Discernment*.

_____
_____
_____
_____
_____
_____
_____
_____
_____
_____
_____
_____
_____
_____
_____
_____
_____
_____
_____
_____
_____
_____
_____
_____
_____
_____
_____
_____
_____
_____

Date:	**Workshop Notes**	Session Number:
Workshop Title _____		Speaker _____

_____

_____

_____

_____

_____

_____

_____

_____

_____

_____

_____

_____

_____

_____

_____

_____

_____

_____

_____

_____

_____

_____

_____

_____

_____

_____

_____

_____

_____

_____

_____

_____

_____

Date:	**Workshop Notes**	Session Number:

Workshop Title _____   Speaker _____

Date:	**Workshop Notes**	Session Number:
Workshop Title _____		Speaker _____

Date: **Workshop Notes** Session Number:

Workshop Title _____   Speaker _____

_____
_____
_____
_____
_____
_____
_____
_____
_____
_____
_____
_____
_____
_____
_____
_____
_____
_____
_____
_____
_____
_____
_____
_____
_____
_____
_____
_____
_____
_____

Date: **Workshop Notes** Session Number:

Workshop Title _____ Speaker _____

Date:	**Workshop Notes**	Session Number:
Workshop Title _____		Speaker _____

Date:	**Workshop Notes**	Session Number:

Workshop Title _____   Speaker _____

_____
_____
_____
_____
_____
_____
_____
_____
_____
_____
_____
_____
_____
_____
_____
_____
_____
_____
_____
_____
_____
_____
_____
_____
_____
_____
_____
_____
_____
_____
_____
_____
_____
_____
_____
_____
_____
_____

Date:	**Workshop Notes**	Session Number:

Workshop Title _____   Speaker _____

_____
_____
_____
_____
_____
_____
_____
_____
_____
_____
_____
_____
_____
_____
_____
_____
_____
_____
_____
_____
_____
_____
_____
_____
_____
_____
_____
_____
_____
_____
_____
_____
_____

Date:	**Workshop Notes**	Session Number:
Workshop Title _____		Speaker _____

_____
_____
_____
_____
_____
_____
_____
_____
_____
_____
_____
_____
_____
_____
_____
_____
_____
_____
_____
_____
_____
_____
_____
_____
_____
_____
_____
_____
_____
_____
_____
_____
_____

Workshop Notes

Date:

Session Number:

Workshop Title _____

Speaker _____

_____
_____
_____
_____
_____
_____
_____
_____
_____
_____
_____
_____
_____
_____
_____
_____
_____
_____
_____
_____
_____
_____
_____
_____
_____
_____
_____
_____
_____
_____
_____
_____
_____
_____
_____
_____
_____

Date:	**Workshop Notes**	Session Number:
Workshop Title _____		Speaker _____

_____

_____

_____

_____

_____

_____

_____

_____

_____

_____

_____

_____

_____

_____

_____

_____

_____

_____

_____

_____

_____

_____

_____

_____

_____

_____

_____

_____

_____

_____

_____

_____

_____

_____

_____

_____

_____

Date:	**Workshop Notes**	Session Number:

Workshop Title _____   Speaker _____

_____
_____
_____
_____
_____
_____
_____
_____
_____
_____
_____
_____
_____
_____
_____
_____
_____
_____
_____
_____
_____
_____
_____
_____
_____
_____
_____
_____
_____
_____
_____
_____
_____
_____
_____

Workshop Notes

Workshop Title _____

Speaker _____

Date:	**Workshop Notes**	Session Number:

Workshop Title _____   Speaker _____

Date:	**Workshop Notes**	Session Number:
Workshop Title _____		Speaker _____

_____
_____
_____
_____
_____
_____
_____
_____
_____
_____
_____
_____
_____
_____
_____
_____
_____
_____
_____
_____
_____
_____
_____
_____
_____
_____
_____
_____
_____
_____

Date:	**Workshop Notes**	Session Number:
Workshop Title _____		Speaker _____

_____
_____
_____
_____
_____
_____
_____
_____
_____
_____
_____
_____
_____
_____
_____
_____
_____
_____
_____
_____
_____
_____
_____
_____
_____
_____
_____
_____
_____

Workshop Notes

Date:

Session Number:

Workshop Title _____

Speaker _____

_____
_____
_____
_____
_____
_____
_____
_____
_____
_____
_____
_____
_____
_____
_____
_____
_____
_____
_____
_____
_____
_____
_____
_____
_____
_____
_____
_____
_____
_____
_____
_____
_____

Workshop Notes

Date:

Session Number:

Workshop Title _____

Speaker _____

Date:	**Workshop Notes**	Session Number:

Workshop Title _____   Speaker _____

_____
_____
_____
_____
_____
_____
_____
_____
_____
_____
_____
_____
_____
_____
_____
_____
_____
_____
_____
_____
_____
_____
_____
_____
_____
_____
_____
_____

www.ingramcontent.com/pod-product-compliance
Lightning Source LLC
LaVergne TN
LVHW081320060426
835509LV00015B/1610